Digger and Lew

Malachy Doyle
Illustrated by
Daniel Howarth

Copyright © QEB Publishing, Inc. 2008

Published in the United States by
QEB Publishing, Inc.
23062 La Cadena Drive
Laguna Hills, CA 92653

www.qeb-publishing.com

A CIP record for this book is available from the Library of Congress.

ISBN 978 1 59566 871 4

Author Malachy Doyle
Illustrator Daniel Howarth
Editor Clare Weaver
Designer Alix Wood
Consultant Anne Faundez

Publisher Steve Evans
Creative Director Zeta Davies

Printed and bound in China

Digger and Lew

Malachy Doyle

Illustrated by
Daniel Howarth

QEB Publishing

QEB

The sun was bright, the bees were buzzing, and Digger, the mole, popped up from under the ground.

He was right in the middle of the cabbage patch,
and who was there, but Lollopy Lew, the hare.

"What are you doing here, on your fat little legs?" said Lollopy Lew.

"Have you come to take over my cabbage patch?"

"There's food enough for both of us," squeaked Digger, blinking at the daylight.

"And my legs are as good as yours any day."

"Under the ground, they are," said Digger, crossly.
"And if you're still here in half an hour, I'll prove it."

"My darling, my dear, I need your help,"
said Digger to Mrs. Digger,
when he got down to his nest.

"For it's time we taught that long-legged hare a lesson."

So they huddled and they muttered...

and they plotted and they planned.

"Are you fit?"
said Digger.

"I'm fit,"
said Lew.

"Are you fast?"
said Digger.

"I'm faster than you!"
said Lew.

"We'll see about that,"
said Digger.
"Now, 1,2,3, go!"

So the hare took off like his tail was on fire, but the mole just popped back under the ground and nibbled a tasty worm.

Yes, Lollopy Lew, he took off like a rocket.
Lollopy Lew, he ran like the wind.

But when he arrived at the
end of the row of cabbages,
up popped a mole.

Beat you!

Poor old Lollopy Lew couldn't believe his eyes.
Beaten by a dumpy little mole!

"I'll get you the next time," said Lollopy Lew,
and he turned and dashed back again.

So, Lollopy Lew bounded back to the bottom of the row. But someone was already there...

"You win," said Lollopy Lew, gasping for breath.
"Your legs are as good as mine."

"Are they better?"
said Digger.

So up at one end of the row, there's Digger, digging up his favorite food.

And down at the other end, there's Mrs. Digger, tucking into hers.

And in the middle, there's Lollopy Lew, nibbling cabbage.

And he never guessed that Mrs. Digger helped Digger to win the race.

Did you?

Notes for teachers and parents

In the story, the moles are called Digger and Mrs. Digger. Ask the children to choose some animals, then give each animal a name that goes with what it does. For example, a dog could be called Barker and a cat Mouser.

The hare is called Lollopy Lew because of how he runs. Ask the children to think of a word that they could use to describe themselves, starting with the same letter as their own name. For example, Clever Chris, Tidy Tom.

What is Lollopy Lew's and Digger's favorite food? Together, make a list of other animals' favorite food.

Ask the children what their favorite food is. See which food is the most popular. Is it the same for boys as it is for girls? Get them to ask some adults what their favorite foods are.

We eat cabbages. Do the children know what other food we eat that grows in the ground?

We don't eat worms, but most of us do eat other living creatures. Ask the children to make a list of other animals that people eat. You could also discuss why some people choose not to eat other living creatures.

Moles live underground. Ask the children to imagine what it would be like to live underground, in the dark.

Make a pretend underground tunnel by covering tables and chairs. Then, in pairs, get the children to act out being Digger and Mrs. Digger, discussing how to get their own back on Lollopy Lew.

Make hand puppets of the three main characters out of old gloves, socks, or paper bags. Help the children to draw or stick on eyes, a nose, and ears. The children can then use the puppets to renact the story.

In the story there are lots of ways to say "went very fast," to describe how Lollopy Lew runs. Can the children tell you what they are? Can they think of any more? What ways could you say went very slowly?

Discuss the story with the children. Why did Lew not want Digger in the cabbage patch? Why did Digger and Mrs. Digger decide to teach him a lesson? What did they decide to do? Why did Lollopy Lew not know there were two moles? How can we tell from the pictures?

Pretend to be Lew and tell the story from his point of view. For example, "I was down in the cabbage patch, minding my own business, when who should pop up right next to me but that naughty little mole." The children can join in and contribute to the story as it progresses. Then tell the story from Digger's point of view.

With two other children, act out the whole story. Move and talk in the way you think the animals would. Afterward, discuss how it felt to be the characters.

Do the children feel sorry for Lollopy Lew? Discuss whether they think the moles were right to trick him. Have the children ever tricked someone? What did they do, and why?